# A SONG & A PRAYER

# A SONG & A PRAYER

30 Devotions Inspired by My Favorite Songs

# LORETTA LYNN

and Kim McLean

New York • Nashville

Worthy
Hachette Book Group
1290 Avenue of the Americas, New York, NY 10104
worthypublishing.com
twitter.com/worthypub

First Edition: May 2023

Worthy is a division of Hachette Book Group, Inc. The Worthy name and logo are trademarks of Hachette Book Group, Inc.

The publisher is not responsible for websites (or their content) that are not owned by the publisher.

Worthy Books may be purchased in bulk for business, educational, or promotional use. For information, please contact your local bookseller or the Hachette Book Group Special Markets Department at special.markets@hbgusa.com.

Scripture quotations are from New Revised Standard Version Bible, copyright © 1989 National Council of the Churches of Christ in the United States of America. Used by permission. All rights reserved worldwide.

Print book interior design by Bart Dawson

Library of Congress Control Number: 2022057841

ISBNs: 978-1-5460-0421-9 (hardcover), 978-1-5460-0422-6 (ebook)

Printed in the United States of America

LSC-C

Printing 1, 2023

*This book is dedicated to our Lord and Savior Jesus Christ, and to all the people in this world who are helping to spread the good news of His love.*

# CONTENTS

# CONTENTS

# INTRODUCTION

It was the most natural thing in the world. We were just talking, and then we were praying, and then we were writing a song. It was all the same to us. I didn't feel time passing during that first impromptu cowrite, but I felt like I'd danced around in eternity with a friend. It felt childlike and free, humble and holy, creative, professional, and...significant. I took the significance to be only for that moment, for that memory, and I was grateful that God had allowed me to become Loretta's friend and prayer partner. It was a way for her to have church without an awestruck crowd around. Not that she doesn't know how to embrace an awestruck crowd and make everyone in it feel like they are the only one there and like she loves them the most. It's because she's so honest. She can't hide a thing. She tells it like it is and sets you straight if she sees you're not doing the same. When you feel her love, it is because she is overflowing with the love she shares with the One who *is* love. God is love, and Loretta Lynn will tell you so.

Our very first conversation swirled around every topic, from a husband-stealing rodeo hussy, to the sorrow of losing a child, to thieves on the cross talking to Jesus about hope. We read the Bible some, shared Communion with the wafers and Welch's I'd brought with me, and then I anointed her forehead and hands with some sweet-smelling anointing oil as we prayed. She loved the oil so much she wanted more of it on the backs of her hands. Later she told me she smelled good for days afterward.

Our first cowrite was a sad country song. She asked me how I was, and I blabbed everything. I had a newly broken heart, and I figured there was no use hiding it from the Queen of Country, so I didn't; and I'm so glad. It was the most healing pity party I've ever had, and in a matter of minutes she somehow gave me the courage to move on *and* we got a great song out of it! After that, we kept writing regularly. We talked about how it is *all* God's music and how every song is a gift from Heaven if you know how to listen for them. There was something special about how the prayers themselves started turning into songs, and that's how we ended up with a few gospel songs. Don't get me wrong, a sad country song is its own kind of prayer. It tells the truth and cries out for love, and God is love. But a prayer with a melody is another matter, and that is what gave us the idea for this book.

Loretta kept telling me she wished the whole world knew how much God loves them. She said God was always with her. She talked to Him all the time and made sure to talk out loud if anyone was around when she happened to be praying so that they would know they can talk to God, too.

When I was talking, laughing, writing, and praying with Loretta, I would think about how one little coal miner's daughter wanted to write and sing, and the whole world is better because of it. She owned it! But she owned it as a gift received, not a status. She said everything she had was because of God.

This book is a thirty-day devotional we've created so you can be a part of a very special kind of prayer meeting. Loretta's wit and wisdom and her profound love for God shine through in her songs, so we've put together a month's worth of encouragement you can use for your spiritual practice morning, noon, or night. Each devotion is inspired by one of Loretta's lyrics that come straight from the heart and real life.

We love you, and we hope this book reminds you that God loves you more than you could even imagine, and He is with you all the time. May your soul sing today.

—*Rev. Kim McLean, EdD*

# DAY 1

# A SONG
# AND
# A PRAYER

❧

Consider the lilies of the field, how they
grow; they neither toil nor spin, yet
I tell you, even Solomon in all his glory
was not clothed like one of these.

Matthew 6:28–29

Most people don't stop to smell the roses. They're too busy worrying about everything. People are the same in every generation; they just find new things to worry over. Times may change, but people don't. It boils down to every human being on God's green earth wanting to feel safe and important, which boils down to everybody wanting to be loved. The thing is, you can't get what you already have. So, chasing love around in all the wrong places is a lot like a dog chasing its tail. The truth is that God loves every single person the same, and He takes care of us all with tender loving care when we let Him. All you have to do is accept the amazing love that has been there for you all along.

It's okay to want to do great things in this world. We should give our very best every day and help people along the way whenever we can. But the secret is this— you don't have to do things to make life worth living; you do things because life *is* worth living, and the only *real* way to live it is with God. When you know in your heart that you are a beautiful rose in love's garden, you are a melody in God's heart, you are a praise to the One who made you, then your life shows it. Consider the lilies, like Jesus said. The lilies in the field just soak in the blessings of the sun, the rain, and the good soil, and God takes care of the rest. God is experiencing His own glory through them, and He wants to do the same through you, and through me.

A good way to start seeing yourself and your life through God's eyes is to pray. God listens and He speaks. Prayer is a conversation. We're all only human, and that's not shameful. You don't ever need to hide from God. Nobody can hide from God. In Psalm 139, King David wrote, "Where can I go from Your Spirit, and where can I flee from your Presence?" God made us, so He could love us and be with us, and it makes His heart sing when we talk to Him. That's the best way to stop and smell the roses. Pray. Pour out your heart. Keep it real and tell God the truth you feel because He knows it anyway.

You don't have to try to be something special in God's eyes, because you already *are* something special.

Give your heart to Jesus and let Him take care of your burdens. When you stop worrying about this, that, and forever, your soul will open up and sing!

## PRAYER FOR TODAY

Lord, thank You for all the many blessings
You have given to me. I'm grateful for every
single one. Help me to show my love for
You today by loving others and by singing
the song You put in my heart. Amen.

# LYRICS
# "A SONG AND A PRAYER"

If I could find the perfect prayer
I would search my soul so deep
Just to have a way to say to You
Lord, how much You mean to me
The only way I've made it through this world
Is by Your tender loving care
You're so close right now
Hope is all around in a song and a prayer

[Chorus]
*So I sing to You and let my heart shine through*
*May my voice reach Heaven's gates*
*It's just a melody that You gave to me*
*Full of joy and full of grace*
*Spirit like a dove carry all my love*
*To the lamb of God so fair*
*With this life I live my most precious gift*
*Is a song and a prayer*

Every prayer is like a butterfly
So fragile yet so strong
When I feel You drawing close to me
I know You've been there all along
I get on my knees to talk to You
But my soul can't help but sing
My song takes flight in Your Holy Light
And flies away on angels' wings

[Chorus]
*So I sing to You and let my heart shine through*
*May my voice reach Heaven's gates*
*It's just a melody that You gave to me*
*Full of joy and full of grace*
*Spirit like a dove carry all my love*
*To the lamb of God so fair*
*With this life I live my most precious gift*
*Is a song and a prayer*

Written by Loretta Lynn and Kim McLean
© Coal Miners Music, Inc./Kim McLean Music

# COAL MINER'S DAUGHTER

If your enemies are hungry, feed them;
if they are thirsty, give them something
to drink; for by doing this you will
heap burning coals on their heads.
Do not be overcome by evil but
overcome evil with good.

Romans 12:20–21

Some people like this Bible verse for all the wrong reasons. It seems like it's saying you can get even by being nice and get away with having the same bitter heart as your enemy. But it ain't sayin' that. When they pass out the halos in Heaven, God is going to know which good deeds were done with a pure heart and which ones were done just to get a score settled.

Heaping burning coals on someone's head sounds terrible. God would never ask us to do such a thing. Songwriters know words are symbols, and a burning coal represents the purifying value of a guilty conscience. If you do something wrong, you ought to do something about it. You get on your knees and ask God to forgive you and help you do better. Then you tell your brother or sister the same thing you told God. That's how you keep a clean heart.

The Bible talks about God's refining fire. In the book of Isaiah, there's even a story of an angel who uses a hot coal to cleanse a prophet's words. If we do what Jesus said and don't judge others, we can always be brave enough to look in the mirror and let the Spirit teach us through our trials and mistakes. The roughest times make the best people if they trust in the Good Lord's grace and forgiveness.

Lord knows we get every opportunity to be mad enough to heap a few coals! But coal also brings warmth and new energy into a room. If we could all learn to heap love onto one another, the world would be a happier place. Let God do the purifying. God is like the coal miner and we're all His children. God will take care of you and me if we keep our eyes on Him.

# PRAYER FOR TODAY

Lord, help me to love others like You do,
even those who hurt me. Keep me safe
from harm, but especially guard my heart
from bitterness and negative feelings.
I will keep my eyes on You, and *You*
keep an eye on them! Amen.

# LYRICS
## "COAL MINER'S DAUGHTER"

Well, I was born a coal miner's daughter
In a cabin, on a hill in Butcher Holler
We were poor but we had love
That's the one thing that daddy made sure of
He shoveled coal to make a poor man's dollar

My daddy worked all night in the Van Lear coal mines
All day long in the field a hoein' corn
Mommy rocked the babies at night
And read the Bible by the coal oil light
And ever' thing would start all over come break of morn

Daddy loved and raised eight kids on a miner's pay
Mommy scrubbed our clothes on a washboard ever' day
Why I've seen her fingers bleed
To complain, there was no need
She'd smile in Mommy's understanding way

In the summertime we didn't have shoes to wear
But in the wintertime, we'd all get a brand-new pair
From a mail order catalog
Money made from selling a hog
Daddy always managed to get the money somewhere

Yeah, I'm proud to be a coal miner's daughter
I remember well, the well where I drew water
The work we done was hard
At night we'd sleep 'cause we were tired
I never thought of ever leaving Butcher Holler

Well a lot of things have changed since a way back then
And it's so good to be back home again
Not much left but the floor, nothing lives here anymore
Except the memory of a coal miner's daughter

Written by Loretta Lynn
© Sure Fire Music Company, Inc.

# EVERYBODY WANTS TO GO TO HEAVEN

Turn back, and say to Hezekiah prince of
my people, Thus, says the Lord, the God
of your ancestor David: I have heard your
prayer, I have seen your tears; indeed,
I will heal you; on the third day you shall
go up to the house of the LORD.
I will add fifteen years to your life.

2 Kings 20:5–6

Hezekiah was the thirteenth king of Judah. He loved God and he loved his people. He had it all, so maybe it was no wonder that when he got sick to the point of death, he cried out to God not to take him. Well, God sent the prophet Isaiah to tell the king He was going to heal him and give him fifteen more years. Hezekiah wanted a sign that he was healed, so God gave him a sign. He turned back time, just for Hezekiah. He just stuck him right in a new time zone.

Nobody wants to die. It means your time is up. But God wanted to show Hezekiah that time belongs to Him. Time is never up when you walk with God. Time on earth reflects eternity, and eternity means time never ends. But don't feel bad if you don't want to die. Even Jesus didn't want to die when He prayed in the Garden, so it must not be a sin, because Jesus never sinned. It's okay to wish you didn't have to go through hard things, but we all do. Nobody wants to die. The important thing is to remember that God sees your tears just like He saw Hezekiah's tears. He knows life on earth is hard sometimes. That's why He went through it with us. God knows how you feel.

Jesus said, "I am the Resurrection and the Life, and he who believes in me will live even though he dies." There is a promise that we can carry around with us that if we believe in Him, we will live even though we die, in eternity with God and our loved ones. Can you hear Jesus asking you today, "Do you believe this?"

# PRAYER FOR TODAY

Dear Lord, help me to cherish this day as a precious gift from You. Help me not to live in fear but to live knowing that life never really ends. Help me to encourage someone else today to believe in You, too, so that they can have the reassurance that they will be in Heaven one day. Amen.

# LYRICS
# "EVERYBODY WANTS TO GO TO HEAVEN"

Everybody wants to go to Heaven
but nobody wants to die
Once upon a time there lived a man
and his name was Hezekiah
He walked with God both day and night
but he didn't wanna die
He cried oh Lord please let me live—
death is close I know
God smiled down on Hezekiah
and give him fifteen years to go

[Chorus]
*Everybody wants to go to Heaven but nobody wants to die*
*Lord I wanna go to Heaven, but I don't wanna die*
*But I long for the day when I'll have new birth*
*Still I love livin' here on earth*

*Everybody wants to go to Heaven but nobody wants to die*

When Jesus lived here on this earth
He knew His father's plan
He knew that He must give His life to save
the soul of man
When Judas had betrayed Him,
His father heard Him cry
He was brave until His death
but He didn't wanna die

[Chorus]
*Everybody wants to go to Heaven but nobody wants to die*
*Lord, I wanna go to Heaven, but I don't wanna die*
*But I long for the day when I'll have new birth*
*Still I love livin' here on earth*
*Everybody wants to go to Heaven but nobody wants to die*

Written by Loretta Lynn
© Sure Fire Music Company, Inc.

# THE WORLD IS IN GOD'S HANDS

All these things my hand has made,
and so all these things are mine,
says the LORD.

Isaiah 66:2

Nobody can take the place of God. He made everything and it's all His. The Bible says that all Heaven declares His glory. When Job was hurting so bad he could barely hang on, God told him not to question. God said, "Where were you when I laid the foundations of the world?" God made the first morning stars sing together. We don't have to question why bad things happen in this world when we know it's in God's hands. He knows everything you have ever been through, and He cares about you. You can trust Him.

It's God who can meet your every need. Nobody can take the place of God in your life when you trust Him. Sure, we all need one another, but it is God who fills our deepest needs. He helps us to help each other in a way that is balanced with love, joy, peace, patience, kindness, generosity, faithfulness, gentleness, and self-control. Those attributes are the fruits of the Spirit, and they grow from the inside out. The more fruit we grow, the better the world will be.

I wish people didn't do bad things to each other.

Love is so simple. Fear is so complicated. People are mean because they are afraid—afraid they're going to miss out. People who make choices that harm others are planting the wrong kind of seed in their minds, in their hearts, and in their lives, so the wrong kind of fruit grows. But *nobody* can take the place of God. We are *all* under God's power and serving God's divine plan. Ain't that gonna get the devil's goat one of these days!

God is in control and you don't have to be anxious about a thing. It's going to be all right. When you press in close to God's heart through prayer, the Bible, and faithful people, you'll be reminded of this truth all the time. There is true peace for those who trust in the Lord.

## PRAYER FOR TODAY

Lord, sometimes I get anxious and
depressed. It's not that I don't trust You.
I just forget, I guess. Please stay close
to me today. Take away my fear and keep
me near to Your heart. Amen.

# LYRICS
# "THE WORLD IS IN GOD'S HANDS"

I've traveled down many a road
And I've learned things along the way
Some days it don't seem worth gettin' up
And some days it just don't pay
But I've learned not to worry and fret
Even when I just don't understand
Cause when you give it one more thought, friend
You know it's in God's hands!

[Chorus]
*Well the world is in God's hands*
*Oh the world is in God's hands*
*You can travel all over this land*
*And you'll see the world is in God's hands*

Well I don't know what you believe
And we might not believe the same

But I feel God with me all the time

Through the sunshine and the rain

They talk like the world is an awful place

Now you know that's just not true

I can't deny the joy I feel inside

From all the hurt He's brought me through

[Chorus]

*Well the world is in God's hands*

*Oh the world is in God's hands*

*You can travel all over this land*

*And you'll see the world is in God's hands*

Written by Loretta Lynn and Kim McLean
© Coal Miners Music, Inc./Kim McLean Music

# DAY 5

# GOD HAS
# A HEART, TOO

❧

**God is love.**

1 John 4:8

I think about God all the time and I see Him everywhere. I don't know how anybody wouldn't know God. He made the mountains. He put all the water in the ocean and told the moon to pull the tide. God knew what He was doing when He made all these things. It's easy to be awestruck in God's presence, when you know He is the One behind all of creation. God is sovereign, all-knowing, all-powerful, and greater than everything. He deserves our respect. But He longs for our love. When people don't respect and love God, they don't love each other very well either, because God designed us to be love. He made love. He gave love. He lived love to show us how to live when He came to earth through Jesus His son.

Respect and love go together. You respect what you love; you love what you respect.

I think a lot of people figure that God made everything, but they don't give it much thought after that. I guess they're scared to look at something so big because then they'll have to realize how small they are. It amazes me every day how such a wise God can love me so much. And He loves you. He knows your name, how many hairs are on your head, and He cares about every breath you take. God didn't make everything so He could love it; He made everything because He *is* love. All of creation, including me and you, is just love spillin' out of Heaven and turning into butterflies and horses, flowers and friends, family and music. He may have the whole world in His hands, but He holds me and you in His heart.

## PRAYER FOR TODAY

Dear Lord, I can only love You with the love
You pour into my heart. Pour in buckets full
today and help me to show Your heart to
everyone I talk to today. Amen.

# LYRICS
## "GOD HAS A HEART, TOO"

I know God can move the mountains
He hung the stars up in the sky
Put the water in the ocean
And told the moon to pull the tide
With just a whisper He could stop a hurricane
It's so amazing how He still knows my name

[Chorus]
*God has strong arms and He always holds me tight*
*And hears every prayer when I talk to Him at night*
*He made a world full of love for me and you…(because)*
*God has a heart too*

I never understood the reason
People walk around in fear
Doing hurt to one another
Like they don't know that God is near

People blame God for their troubles all the time
But He lets us know that He is only good and kind

[Chorus]
*God has strong arms and He'll always hold you tight*
*And hears every prayer when you talk to Him at night*
*He made a world full of love for me and you…(because)*
*God has a heart too*
*Big enough to give His son*
*To die for us all in spite of all we've done*
*He made a world full of love for me and you*
*God has a heart too*
*Full of love for me and you*
*God has a heart too*

Written by Loretta Lynn and Kim McLean
© Coal Miners Music, Inc./Kim McLean Music

# SOMEBODY ELSE PRAY

Ask, and it will be given you; search,
and you will find; knock, and the door
will be opened for you.

Matthew 7:7

I love going to church, and I sure do love to pray. I pray all the time, because God is always here with me, so it's more like we're just talking. I learned how to pray from my mama and from going to church. I used to love old-time revival meetings where we'd sing the old hymns, hear a great sermon, and then pray. I can still hear the preacher prayin' up a storm and then shoutin', "Now, somebody else pray!!" He wanted us all to have the chance to storm Heaven with our heart's desire. If nobody spoke up, he'd call on a sister or a brother and they'd rise to their feet and stand on the promises with sincere requests. People prayed for the sick, the lost, and the lame. Now and then, even a little child would pray. There was nothin' too big or small to bring to God.

Prayer is powerful. Jesus taught us to pray, so He must want us to do a lot of it. Can you imagine what the world would be like if everybody prayed? Prayer is a connection, like a hotline to Heaven. It's another way to love God and others, maybe the most powerful way.

Jesus wouldn't have said, "Thy will be done on earth as it is in Heaven" if it were not possible, and I believe that's exactly what is happening when we pray. God's will is gettin' done on earth as it is in Heaven.

We may not know exactly what Heaven looks like, but I'm praying for a glimpse of it in my life today. Now, somebody else pray!!

# PRAYER FOR TODAY

Our Father, who art in Heaven, hallowed
be Thy name. Thy kingdom come, Thy will
be done on earth as it is in Heaven.
Give us this day our daily bread and forgive
us our trespasses as we forgive those who
trespass against us. And lead us not into
temptation but deliver us from evil;
for Thine is the kingdom and the power
and the glory forever. Amen.

# LYRICS
## "SOMEBODY ELSE PRAY"

I was sittin' in church on Sunday

In my hometown in Tennessee

We sang a lot of hymns that morning

And God was blessing me

I could feel the Spirit moving

I thought of Jesus on the cross

I cried, "Come and heal the broken,

come and save the one that's lost."

[Chorus]

*Now somebody else pray*

*Keep the gospel goin'*

*Somebody else pray*

*Gotta keep His love a flowin'*

*Pour out your heart now*

*God hears every word you say*

*We got a good thing goin' now*

*Let's keep it that way*

*Somebody else pray*

Turn around and greet your neighbor

We're gathered in His name

Ain't nobody here a stranger

We're so glad you came

Take the hand beside you

And lift up someone in need

Just like Jesus did every day He lived

That's how He taught you and me

[Chorus]

*Now somebody else pray*

*Keep the gospel goin'*

*Somebody else pray*

*Gotta keep His love a flowin'*

*Pour out your heart now*

*God hears every word you say*

*We got a good thing goin' now*

*Let's keep it that way*

*Somebody else pray*

Written by Loretta Lynn and Kim McLean
© Coal Miners Music, Inc./Kim McLean Music

# ELZIE BANKS

For the message about the cross is
foolishness to those who are perishing,
but to us who are being saved
it is the power of God.

1 Corinthians 1:18

Nothing can separate us from God's love (Romans 8:39; paraphrased).

I used to love the old-time gospel preachers. Times have changed, but I wish you could've been there. Preacher Elzie Banks brought the gospel to Butcher Holler. His sermons brought Heaven down and raised a little holy hell, if you know what I mean. When he stepped behind that pulpit, you knew he was going to tell it like it is. Elzie wasn't in it for money or fame. He wasn't trying to get the church to grow. He was trying to get people to love God by livin' right. When you live right, you feel better, the world gets better, and it makes God's heart sing because He only wants the best for His children.

Elzie wasn't afraid of the devil. He said you should never give the devil an inch of your life because he'll go for the whole nine yards. I say there's no such thing as givin' the devil his due, because we don't owe him nothin'—but we owe God everything. When you give your whole life to God, He'll guide you in everything you do, from family, to church, to work, to every place in between.

We may think it's our bad luck or our failures that reward the devil, but the only thing the devil really wants is to steal our love for God. When we give up the joy of loving and trusting God, we lose joy with other people, especially our loved ones and friends. But don't worry. The devil can't take anything you don't give him. So let that ole buzzard work twenty-*five* hours a day if he wants. I'm keepin' my eyes on Jesus and my heart set for Heaven. We'll get a kick out of watching the devil try to set up stumblin' blocks. We'll just stack 'em up and climb a little closer to glory!

# PRAYER FOR TODAY

Lord, please bless all the preachers
and teachers out there today who are
carrying Your gospel message to people.
Give them boldness to speak the truth.
Protect them from falling so they can keep
doing Your work. And, Lord, make me
a minister of Your Word everywhere I go,
even though I'm not a preacher. I want to
let my light shine!!! Amen.

# LYRICS
## "ELZIE BANKS"

There's an old-time preacher named Elzie Banks
and he tells it like it is
He says, "You can't be good if you're a little bit bad,
cause the devil knows you're his."
When he preaches that fire and brimstone,
you can almost see the flames
But when he says you'll walk them golden streets
ten thousand angels sing
He'd break the ice on the river in the middle
of wintertime
And say, "Come on, Sister, wade right in,
the water's mighty mighty fine!"
He'd raise one hand toward the heavens
and then he'd say, "Let's pray.
Come on Lord, we're gonna show this world,
we're gonna drown the ole devil today!"

[Chorus]
*(and we'll say) "Come on children,*
*Let your little light shine high on the mountaintop*
*We'll get a kick out of watching the devil*
*Settin' them stumblin' blocks*
*This world is the devil's playground*
*And I hate like the devil to say*
*He's the hardest worker in this world*
*He works 25 hours a day!*

Preacher Elzie, keep on a preachin' and never
let your people down
I miss the old camp meetin' time and dinner
on the grounds
He's an old-time gospel preacher and he preaches
the gospel free
The mountain people need him, and they love him
just like me
Lord I wouldn't be caught dead without my Jesus
to hold onto

If you don't know your Lord today, tomorrow
He won't know you
Don't get me wrong I believe in givin' I strongly
believe in tithin'
But them TV preachers are losing souls with
bank accounts they're savin'.

[Chorus]
*(and we'll say) "Come on children,*
*Let your little light shine high on the mountaintop*
*We'll get a kick out of watching the devil*
*Settin' them stumblin' blocks*
*This world is the devil's playground*
*Lord, I hate like the devil to say*
*He's the hardest worker in this world*
*He works 25 hours a day!*

Written by Loretta Lynn
© Coal Miners Music, Inc.

# THE THIRD MAN

For God so loved the world that He gave
His only Son, so that everyone
who believes in Him may not perish
but may have eternal life.

John 3:16

Every time I read my Bible, I think about Jesus on the cross and how He died for me. He was the King of Glory who had never done anything wrong, but He was crucified between two thieves. I guess the Roman soldiers had a place on Calvary's hill saved just for Jesus, but they didn't know that Jesus had a spot for them in Heaven if they accepted His forgiveness. Jesus died for everybody. That's how much He loves us. He knows that we can't do any better, so He died to take away our sins. But you've got to believe in Him. You've got to walk right up to that cross and see it for yourself. You've got to let that precious blood drip onto your hand and look right up into His eyes. That's when you'll see that He loves you more than anything.

It will surprise you when you see His face. Jesus never makes you feel ashamed, but you might feel pretty sad when your sin-stained heart is standing next to His pure white grace. When we've done wrong, and we go to Him in humble faith, He never gets angry. You can't shock Jesus. He's seen it all! So, don't be scared to talk to

Him and tell Him everything—and I mean *everything*! You can tell your deepest, darkest secrets to Jesus and He will help you. He will wash you clean and give you the power to resist the temptation to sin. He will fill your life with love. Can you hear Him talking to you today? "I'm doing this for you!"

# PRAYER FOR TODAY

Lord, please give us all the courage to look into Your face and believe in You. Thank You for what You did for us on the cross. Your suffering for us was greater than anything we can imagine, and Your love for us is just as big now as it was back then. Jesus, call to the people in my life who don't know You yet and help them to find Your great forgiveness and love. Amen.

# LYRICS
## "THE THIRD MAN"

Last night I dreamed I took a walk
Up Calvary's lonely hill
The things I saw with my own eyes
Could not have been more real
I saw upon three crosses
Three men in agony
Two cried out for mercy
And a third man looked at me
And oh, the hurt in this man's eyes
Just broke my heart in two
And it seemed that I could hear Him say
"I'm doing this for you."
I knelt beneath the third man's cross
And slowly bowed my head
I reached out to touch His feet
And it stained my hand with red
And when I heard Him cry in pain

I raised my eyes to see
The blood spilled from the third man's side
And some of it spilled on me
The third man wore a crown of thorns
Spikes held Him to the tree
And I heard Him say, "Oh God, My God
Hast Thou forsaken me?"
And there within the mighty crowd
The ones who mocked Him cried
Said, "King, save Thyself if Thou art King!"
And then the third man died
Suddenly, I heard the thunder roar
I saw lightning pierce the sky
The third man was still hanging there
And I began to cry
I saw the boulders fall
And heard the breaking of the ground
Then I awoke
And though I dreamed
I touched my cheek and found

My eyes were wet where I had cried
A dream I wished I knew
I still can hear the third man say
"I'm doing this for you."

Written by Loretta Lynn, Frances Heighton, Teddy Wilbur
© Sure Fire Music Company, Inc.

**DAY 9**

# STANDING ROOM ONLY

As I live, says the Lord, every knee shall
bow to me, and every tongue shall
give praise to God.

Romans 14:11

So that at the name of Jesus every knee
should bend, and every tongue should
confess that Jesus Christ is Lord,
to the glory of God the Father.

Philippians 2:10–11

I've been thinking about Heaven. Once I had a dream that there was standing room only at Heaven's gate as everyone who ever lived answered to God. It made me wake up and pay attention to how much I want to live for Him. I think Heaven must be the happiest place, but if I were there and my loved ones weren't, I'd be there with a broken heart missing them.

I don't think God wants us to try to scare people into Heaven. You win souls by loving people. Hell sounds awful and I don't want to go there, but the real reason I want to go to Heaven is because I like to be close to God. I love God with all my heart.

I also want you to go to Heaven, because I love you with all my heart, too. Or maybe I should say I love you with all God's heart, because He's the one who put this love in me.

I have peace in my heart knowing that one day I'll be in Heaven with Jesus. I don't ever have to be afraid, and you don't have to be, either. Through the cross, God has given us *everlasting* life. All you have to do is accept Jesus into your heart. Just say it straight out: "Jesus, come into my heart," and He'll be there to comfort and guide you. Everlasting life starts now.

The Bible teaches about a judgement day when God will either say to us, "Welcome home, my child," or God will have to say, "You wanted to do things your way— so thy will be done." I think that's what hell is. Hell is getting your own way. People might think they want to be in charge of their own lives, but the only real way to take charge of your life is to give it back to the One who gave it to you in the first place. He can show you how to make the most of it!

## PRAYER FOR TODAY

Jesus, You took on our nature so we could take on Yours. Line my will up with Your will so that my greatest desire is to love like You love. Amen.

# LYRICS
## "STANDING ROOM ONLY"

*Standing room only, not even room to kneel and pray*
*Standing room only on the Judgement Day*

Last night I had an awful dream that the
end of time had come
The trumpet had been sounded and life on
earth was done.
An angel stood, one foot on land the other
foot on sea
And as I tried to kneel and pray a voice
said unto me

*There's standing room only, it's too late now to pray*
*There's standing room only, this is the Judgement Day*

People filled each church and churchyard just as
far as I could see

I heard a pitiful cry for mercy and then I realized
it was me
I saw the Savior then appear as He split
the eastern sky
I saw tears of joy on a Christian's face
and I heard the sinners cry

And as I tried to touch His hand with one
last feeble plea
I cried again have mercy, have mercy Lord on me
The earth was burning all around;
the world went up in smoke
And as the flames came off me, thank God I awoke
Then I got out of bed and I got down on my knees
And you should've heard me pray
For in my dream I witnessed God's great Judgement Day
*Standing room only on God's great Judgement Day*

Written by Loretta Lynn and Frances Heighton
© Sure Fire Music Company, Inc.

## DAY 10

# GOD NEVER GAVE UP ON ME

Now to him who is able to keep you from
falling, and to make you stand without
blemish in the presence of his glory with
rejoicing, to the only God our Savior,
through Jesus Christ our Lord, be glory,
majesty, power, and authority, before
all time and now and forever. Amen.

Jude 24–25

Hard times hurt. That's just all there is to it. Sometimes you get everything right and things still go wrong. You go to church, work hard, do your best, and things fall apart. We all go through it, every one of us. The important thing is what you do with those hard times. Trust in God. He will help you. When the world goes dark, He will be your light. When you can't catch your breath, He will be your air. When you're hungry, He'll feed your soul. Keep your eyes on God and let Him take care of the rest.

God has always taken care of me and my family. We had some pretty rough times when there wasn't enough food on the table. But we made it through by God's grace. God will walk with you every step of the way. He hurts when you hurt, He cries when you cry, and He'll never leave you alone.

I've never found much reason to whine about anything. Everybody goes through something. When you know that God doesn't give up on you, you know that everything is going to be all right. I love the old hymn that says, "It is well with my soul." When it's well with your soul, you can get through anything. Sometimes people get mad at God, but God doesn't put troubles on us. Our trials are only opportunities to remind us that God never gives up on us.

Sometimes we bring trials on ourselves by misbehavin'. A guilty conscience ain't a bad thing when you're actually guilty. It is a compass to lead you back on track. God never gives up on our highest potential for good. He uses His rod to lead us on the right path, just like David used his shepherd's hook to lead the sheep. In the book of Jude, there is a promise that God can keep us from falling. You might stumble now and then, but God will always be there to catch you. There's no such thing as a hopeless case with a God who never gives up!

## PRAYER FOR TODAY

Lord, forgive me for the times I've acted
like You might not take care of me,
and I worried needlessly. Thank You for
the trials, thank You for the good times.
May it all bring me closer to You. Amen.

# LYRICS
## "GOD NEVER GAVE UP ON ME"

I've been through some rough times
And I felt like I could die
Some days I felt so beat up
All I could do was cry
My babies, they were hungry
And I was getting hungry, too
So I called out, Dear Jesus
And you know He helped me through

[Chorus]
*I'll never give up on God*
*Cause God never gave up on me*
*He washed away my sorrows*
*On a cross at Calvary*
*So I'll give Him all the glory*
*And I'll serve Him faithfully*
*I'll never give up on God*
*Cause God never gave up on me*

I don't blame God for my troubles
He knows them every one
He gives me all the grace I need
And strength to carry on
I don't regret a single day
He's been with me through them all
He helps me when I stumble and He'll catch me if I fall

[Chorus]
*I'll never give up on God*
*Cause God never gave up on me*
*He washed away my sorrows*
*On a cross at Calvary*
*So I'll give Him all the glory*
*And I'll serve Him faithfully*
*I'll never give up on God*
*Cause God never gave up on me*

Written by Loretta Lynn and Kim McLean
© Coal Miners Music, Inc./Kim McLean Music

# IT IS WELL

Peace I leave with you; my peace I give
to you. I do not give to you as the world
gives. Do not let your hearts be troubled,
and do not let them be afraid.

John 14:27

It would be easy for most people to find about a million reasons to be unhappy about something in this life. Complaining comes natural. It's too hot, too cold, your boots are too tight, and your bills are too due. There are big things, too, things that hurt so bad you think you'll never get over them. When you're sad or angry, that's okay. Tell the truth about it, but don't hang on to it. Let your tears flow like a river, but you know what a river does? It keeps moving. It keeps flowing. It goes someplace new.

It's the deep part of a river that counts the most. That's where the power is. Rapids might look fierce, but it's the current beneath the quiet waters that drives the water to the sea. I think about that every time I sing, "When peace like a river attendeth my way." Having peace is not about what's happening on the surface; it's a deep inside *knowing* that no matter what you're going through, God is with you. When you know that God is with you all the time and everywhere, then it truly is well with your soul all the time. God is good all the time. God can only love us and care for us. It's His nature.

Not too long ago, Alison Krauss sang this beautiful old hymn at my birthday party. It was the prettiest thing you ever heard. She sings like an angel, and I know there were angels all around listenin' and singin' along.

When our faith becomes sight, like this song says, we see angels everywhere. We see love everywhere because God is love and He is everywhere.

The ole devil doesn't stand a chance against somebody who has seen the Lord. I had to stand up to the devil once and let him know that I belong to God and that I only listen to God. Once I told him no, he never came around again. In the Bible, James says to resist the devil and he'll flee from you. And you know, he doesn't walk up to you in a red suit with horns and a long, sharp tail. He might have a sharp tongue, or a silver one (that ole silver-tongued devil)! He'll walk right up to you and offer you his hand, but don't ever take it! You can recognize the devil when God's Spirit warns you that he's around. That's why it is important to draw near to God every single day. Jesus will guide you and keep you safe so that you don't fall prey to any of the devil's schemes. All the devil is after is your joy, the joy in your soul. He probably hates it when we sing this great song. Let him throw a fit. I'll just sing louder!

God is the only one who can truly make you feel that it is well with your soul. Every person has a God-shaped hole in their heart that only God can fill. I'm going to be thinkin' about God's river today and letting that living water Jesus talked about fill me up again. The psalmist said the river of God is *full* of water. Spring up, oh well, within my soul, and let it be well with my soul!

## PRAYER FOR TODAY

Lord, thank You for the way You pay
attention to Your children and to me.
You've given me every good thing that
I have, and You've been with me through
every trial. Be my refuge again today, Lord,
and let me be a testimony of Your love and
grace to someone else today. Amen.

# LYRICS
## "IT IS WELL"

When peace like a river attendeth my way
When sorrows like sea billows roll
Whatever my lot thou hast taught me to say
It is well, it is well with my soul!

[Chorus]
*It is well (it is well)*
*With my soul (with my soul)*
*It is well,*
*It is well with my soul*

Though Satan should buffet, though trials should come
Let this blest assurance control
That Christ hath regarded my helpless estate
And hath shed His own blood for my soul!

[Chorus]
*It is well (it is well)*
*With my soul (with my soul)*
*It is well,*
*It is well with my soul*

My sin, oh the bliss of this glorious thought
My sin, not in part but the whole,
Is nailed to the cross, and I bear it no more
Praise the Lord, praise the Lord, oh my soul.

[Chorus]
*It is well (it is well)*
*With my soul (with my soul)*
*It is well,*
*It is well with my soul*

And Lord haste the day when my faith shall be sight
The clouds be rolled back as a scroll

The trump shall resound and the Lord shall descend

Even so, it is well with my soul!

[Chorus]

*It is well (it is well)*

*With my soul (with my soul)*

*It is well,*

*It is well with my soul*

Horatio Spafford (public domain)

# MY BEST FRIEND

I have called you friends, because
I have made known to you everything
that I have heard from my Father.

John 15:15

I have the best friends in the world. Patsy Cline was one of my closest friends, and you know, me and Conway were close like a brother and sister. But there are so many more it would take up this whole book to tell you. I love everybody and I want everybody to know that God loves them, too. Jesus wants to be your friend.

You know how you know somebody is your friend? They want to be with you. The other day, Chris Stapleton came by, and we had the best time. I just love his music; I listen to him all the time. And Garth Brooks sent me about a million roses not too long ago just to let me know he appreciates me. The whole room was a beautiful garden filled with the scent of Heaven. So many of my friends gathered in Nashville for my birthday at the Bridgestone Arena. Tanya Tucker, Alison Krauss, Brandi Carlile, and my dear friend Jack White were all there with me and my family. And I have a lot of friends you wouldn't know because they're not famous, but they stand by me through thick and thin. I wish you could know 'em. Being famous doesn't make you more special.

It just means a lot of people know who you are. Every person is famous in the eyes of God. I guess you could say God plays favorites, and everybody is His favorite. He wants to be with you all the time.

God wanted to be our friend all along. He went walking with Adam and Eve in the cool of the day, like friends do. And the Bible tells us that Abraham was called a friend of God because his faith was so real. Do you know why it takes faith to be friends with God? It's because God is Spirit. You sense His presence. You hear His voice in a thought that comes to mind or an inspiration that whispers by. Most of the time He is invisible, but I wouldn't call Him an invisible friend. God is more real than anything, so real these eyes can't take Him all in. I guess God doesn't want to overwhelm us. Moses wanted to know what God looked like, but God only allowed Moses to see His back as He walked by. And the disciples saw their friend Jesus transfigured with white light brighter than any other white on this earth. They were seeing God. Jesus was fully human and fully God.

We can't *fully* understand that idea. But isn't it something that the disciples got to walk with Jesus like a friend, with flesh and bones, all over Jerusalem, and then again as a resurrected Savior and friend on the road to Emmaus? They even ate some grilled fish together on the beach! I wish I could've been there.

Being friends is not just knowing what somebody looks like but is also about connecting with them heart to heart.

Jesus is my best friend. He knows me inside and out and He's with me all the time. I don't know how to explain it, but He's here just as real as those roses Garth sent. He talks to me. He listens to me, and He never has to go home, because He has a home in my heart.

## PRAYER FOR TODAY

Jesus, You've never let me down.
You've walked with me through every valley
and every dark night, and You've been with
me in the good times, too. I love this life
with You. Thank You for being such
a great friend. Amen.

# LYRICS
## "MY BEST FRIEND"

Lord, I love You so much, I feel You with me right now
Let's just sit down and talk for a little while
I'm so blessed by Your touch, and my heart overflows
I'm so grateful that You call me Your child

[Chorus]
*You're my best friend*
*Always holding my hand*
*Every nook and valley we walk through*
*There's a promised land*
*Just around the bend*
*I'm going there with my best friend*

You laid down Your life on the cross for us
I wish everyone everywhere believed
Your love is so great—oh I love You so much
Thank You Father, for all You've done for me

[Chorus]

*You're my best friend*

*Always holding my hand*

*Every nook and valley we walk through*

*There's a promised land*

*Just around the bend*

*I'm going there with my best friend*

Written by Loretta Lynn and Kim McLean
© Coal Miners Music, Inc./Kim McLean Music

# A BETTER
# WAY TO SAY
# GOODBYE

As God's chosen ones, holy and beloved,
clothe yourselves with compassion,
kindness, humility, meekness,
and patience.

Colossians 3:12

Nobody likes to say goodbye. It always means you're about to miss somebody you love. It's easier when you know they'll be back soon, and harder when you know they won't, but there's a different kind of hurt when somebody you love says goodbye in a mean way.

Some things in life are a given. Everything changes, and everyone says goodbye. So many things are out of our control, but one thing you *can* control is how you treat other people. You don't have to like everybody. You might not be able to stay in a bad relationship, but if you do the leavin', do it the kindest way you can. If you're the one gettin' left, cry your tears, let it go, and move on, but don't let bitterness grow in your heart. That will hurt you more than it hurts them. Jesus told us to love our enemy, and God says vengeance belongs to Him. Just get on with your life and trust that everything will be okay.

Endings are part of life.

The way you do anything is the way you do everything. If you walk through this life treating others with dignity and grace, you'll even look at those who hurt you with dignity and grace, although you might not invite them over for dinner! But the Bible says to be wise as a serpent and harmless as a dove.

If you've ever had somebody fool you by tellin' you they loved you when they really didn't, don't ever feel ashamed about that. That's on them. Shame on people who take advantage of innocent hearts. The important thing to know is that God will take care of you through everything. Jesus knew about rejection better than anything. It breaks my heart when I think about the crown of thorns on His head, and all the other cruel things they did just to try and get rid of Him. If you've been hurt and rejected, Jesus is sayin' to you today, "I've been there, too." He knows your every sorrow, and that's why He can comfort your heart. The Lord will remind you of how precious you are until you believe it again. He'll wait up with you through the sleepless nights until you wake up knowing that you are as beautiful and awesome as you ever were before somebody hurt you.

You know the best way to finally say goodbye in your

own heart to someone who's treated you bad? Get happy again. If it's somebody you loved, you'll carry a place in your heart for them, but get on with livin'. Don't give them another thought, and if the thought comes anyway, shoo it away like an ole horsefly. Don't let a mean person rob you of sharing good times with the people who really love you.

One other thing. There's more good in this world than bad. You're not bad or dumb for trusting the wrong person. You're just a loving person. Now you've learned. You might get hurt again, but it won't be as bad because you'll be stronger. As you learn to trust yourself again, you'll find that there are still plenty of trustworthy people like you in this world.

## PRAYER FOR TODAY

Dear Lord, please heal the broken places
in my life and make every crooked path
straight. Heal my heart to love again
and send people into my life who
will respect and cherish me the way
I deserve to be loved. Amen.

# LYRICS
## "A BETTER WAY TO SAY GOODBYE"

You could've left a letter on the table
Could've tacked a note up on the door
It would've hurt bad then but by now I'd be okay
Surely there was one kind word you could've found
But you never even tried
There must be a better way to say goodbye

[Chorus]
*For you love never happened*
*You had me fooled right from the start*
*I gave you everything I had*
*But you walked all over my heart*
*There's a million things you could've done*
*Think you tried 'em all on me*
*There must be*
*A better way to say goodbye*

I didn't know you were unhappy
Heard it from everybody else
I could've never ever made you hurt like this
Gettin' over you won't be so easy
I'm runnin' out of places to hide and cry
There must be a better way to say goodbye

[Chorus]
*For you love never happened*
*You had me fooled right from the start*
*I gave you everything I had*
*But you walked all over my heart*
*There's a million things you could've done*
*Think you tried 'em all on me*
*There must be*
*A better way to say goodbye*

[TAG]
There must be a better way to say goodbye

Written by Loretta Lynn and Kim McLean
© Coal Miners Music, Inc./Kim McLean Music

# AMAZING GRACE

As far as the east is from the west,
so far he removes our
transgressions from us.

Psalm 103:12

Sometimes I talk to God and tell Him I'm sorry for the things I've done wrong. There are some things I wish I hadn't done, but I did 'em and I can't change that now. God never holds those things against me, and He won't hold your sins against you, if you tell Him you're sorry and try to stop the sin. I've heard some people say they can't help it if they sin, but they really can; they just don't want to. It's easier to blame stuff on being human, but God helps us. So, we have no excuse. Sin just means "missing the mark." When you shoot an arrow with a bow, you might miss the bull's-eye. That's what sin is. Missing the best God has for you. Sometimes we have to pray for better aim—and don't forget that practice makes perfect.

The most important thing is to know that God loves you no matter what. You can't do anything to make God stop loving you. He always wants what's best for you, like a parent does a child.

Once you know you are forgiven, God's love and grace keep you motivated to live right. If you think you don't have the willpower, God will help you. God is *so* good. He forgives our mistakes, but He gives us the power to stop making the same mistakes. As soon as you ask for His help, you've surrendered your heart to Him a little more. A heart that belongs to God beats with God's love. Then you only want what's best for yourself and others. You want what God wants.

Have you ever noticed verses two and three of this *amazing* song "Amazing Grace"? They are not about grace from sin, but grace through hard times, and grace to overcome our fears. I think people forget about that sometimes when they're singing this song. It's not so much a song about us as it is a song about God. It's a song full of gratitude and praise for the One who watches over us and helps us through every trial. It's a reminder to notice the miracle in every sunrise, on every rose petal, in every melody that spills out of a country singer's soul.

I think we get hung up on the word *amazing*. We think it has to be big and loud and unusual. But the most unusual thing in the world these days is peace of mind.

Anybody can be part of a big roarin' crowd, but who else but God can whisper with a still small voice and still cut through the noise to get to your heart? *That's* amazing. No wonder the psalmist said we should be still and know that He is God.

God is not looking for what's wrong with us; He's looking to help us. He's looking at what's right with us because He created us in His image, and by His grace, through Christ, He's helping us live up to it...every day.

## PRAYER FOR TODAY

Dear Lord, help me to look for what's right more than I look for what's wrong in this world or in my life. Open my eyes today to the beauty and love all around. Open my heart to pray for those who are lost, or addicted, or scared. Most of all, help us all to be still enough to notice Your amazing grace today. Amen.

# LYRICS
## "AMAZING GRACE"

Amazing grace how sweet the sound
That saved a wretch like me
I once was lost but now I'm found
Was blind but now I see

'Twas grace that taught my heart to fear
And grace my fears relieved
How precious did that grace appear
The hour I first believed

Through many dangers toils and snares
I have already come
'Tis grace that brought me safe thus far
And grace will lead me home

When we've been there ten thousand years
Bright shining as the sun
We've no less days to sing God's praise
Than when we first begun

Written by John Newton (public domain)

# DAY 15

# LONG TIME
# LEAVIN'

❧

The Lord is near to the brokenhearted,
and saves the crushed in spirit.

Psalm 34:18

I miss my late husband, Doo, all the time. I always will till I die and I'm with him in Heaven. When you lose somebody you love, whether they pass from this earth or you break up, it hurts, and if you really loved 'em, it's always going to hurt. That doesn't mean you don't move on in life. But it can take a long time to leave the memories back where they belong so you can get on with livin' again. Sometimes you just have to act like you're gonna make it until your heart catches up. When you can't change what is happening, it won't do any good to stay stuck in it.

You have to be patient with memories. They're tricky. Bad memories hurt, but good memories hurt worse because you start wanting those times back and you have to let go all over again. I like to turn those memories into songs. It gets it out and lets me move on. It lets the whole world feel the feelings with me and maybe helps people work through some of their own heartaches as well. Not everybody writes songs like me, but everybody can do something to help themselves heal and maybe bless somebody else in the process. There are times when you just have to get by yourself and shake your fist at Heaven until you feel God take you by the hand to get you across a grand canyon of sorrow.

Your memories tell your story. You can't just throw 'em all away. But they're not the whole story. You'll learn to cherish them with gratitude for the life you've lived. All the little things, like photographs and favorite shows, coffee mugs and whatnots from every town, dishes that made it through every move, and the lucky horseshoe over the door...so many things that once brought smiles can open a floodgate of tears when you miss somebody.

How do you go on? You trust in God's promise to be near you. He is extra near to the brokenhearted. He catches every tear. He sees your crushed spirit and you can cry on His shoulder for as long as it takes. He will comfort your soul in so many ways, with a verse, a song, a friend, or a thousand other things that come just at the right moment when you need it the most. He will strengthen you to get on with your life. He will help you focus on other things. Leave those cares with Jesus and when a hard memory comes up, hand it to Him then and there.

## PRAYER FOR TODAY

Lord, my heart hurts so bad sometimes
I think I can hardly go on, but I know that
with Your help I will make it. I'll get through
the valleys because You are with me.
Thank You for walking beside me all the
way, and when I can't take another step,
You carry me through the day. Amen.

# LYRICS
## "LONG TIME LEAVIN'"

I keep comin' across old memories that you gave me
They remind that the love we had was real
I kept a few sweet things that I can't give
you back now
True love is something hearts can always feel

[Chorus]
*It takes a long time leavin'*
*And a long time to forget*
*As long as I'm still breathin'*
*I ain't over you yet*
*It might take another lifetime*
*If it does I won't regret*
*It takes a long time leavin'*
*And  longer to forget*

I wish I could just decide to send you walking
You twisted every tear right out of my heart

And again last night I almost dialed your number
Then I nearly died from wondering where you are

[Chorus]
*It takes a long time leavin'*
*And a long time to forget*
*As long as I'm still breathin'*
*I ain't over you yet*
*It might take another lifetime*
*If it does I won't regret*
*It takes a long time leavin'*
*And longer to forget*

[TAG]
*Love's a long time leavin'*
*And forever to forget*

Written by Loretta Lynn and Kim McLean
© Coal Miners Music, Inc./Kim McLean Music

## DAY 16

# HOW GREAT
# THOU ART

~⊷~

Bless the Lord, O my soul. O Lord
my God, you are very great. You are
clothed with honor and majesty.

Psalm 104:1

Oh Lord, my God." If that great hymn had ended right there, I would have still been blessed by just those four words. It's what the whole song is really about—the awesomeness of knowing God for yourself.

The Bible talks about how great God is. I like to think about how people since the beginning of time starting with Adam and Eve have known how great God is. Human beings have always known that God is great in power, and the ones who dare to give Him another thought find out that He is also great in love. It's amazing to think about how the Creator of the whole universe cares about me like I'm the most important thing in the world. He loves us and it must break His heart when people don't love Him back.

The Bible isn't just about God. It's also about people. Whatever century we are born into, the human heart is still the same. That's why we can read those old Bible stories and relate to them. The scenery may change, but the soul is the same, and God is the same. He is a steady force of true power and wisdom, slow to anger, full of compassion and always present. Isn't it amazing to know that we have a God so great who is taking care of us?

You are safe. You are loved.

I love the way a soul can sing. It means you're not just singin' the notes right—you're singin' the story behind every note. When I write a song, I write it like I'd say it. Then I sing it like I mean it with all my heart. There's no point in writin' or singin' a song if you don't really mean it. Maybe I learned about that from singin' this song "How Great Thou Art" in church. You can't sing this one without meaning it. The way those notes go up on "then sings my soul" makes your soul go right up with 'em. I think we owe God the very best of our soul, just for being such a great God.

## PRAYER FOR TODAY

Oh Lord, my God, I am awed by
Your presence. I know that You are with
me all the time. I am safe. I am loved.
I am Yours. Amen.

# LYRICS
## "HOW GREAT THOU ART"

Oh Lord, my God
When I, in awesome wonder
Consider all the worlds Thy hands have made
I see the stars, I hear the rolling thunder
Thy power throughout the universe displayed

[Chorus]
*Then sings my soul, my Savior God to Thee*
*How great Thou art, how great Thou art*
*Then sings my soul, my Savior God to Thee*
*How great Thou art, how great Thou art*

And when I think that God, His Son not sparing
Sent Him to die, I scarce can take it in
That on the cross, my burden gladly bearing
He bled and died to take away my sin

[Chorus]
*Then sings my soul, my Savior God to Thee*
*How great Thou art, how great Thou art*
*Then sings my soul, my Savior God to Thee*
*How great Thou art, how great Thou art*

When Christ shall come, with shout of acclamation
And take me home, what joy shall fill my heart
Then I shall bow, in humble adoration
And then proclaim, my God, how great Thou art

[Chorus]
*Then sings my soul, my Savior God to Thee*
*How great Thou art, how great Thou art*
*Then sings my soul, my Savior God to Thee*
*How great Thou art, how great Thou art*

Written by Carl Boberg (public domain)

# BEST THING THAT EVER HAPPENED

We also boast in our sufferings, knowing
that suffering produces endurance,
and endurance produces character,
and character produces hope.

Romans 5:3–4

It's hard to understand why we have to suffer, but life is hard sometimes and we can't do a thing about it. You can't keep bad things from happening. Bad things happen to everybody. Bad things happen to good people. Sometimes you pray and pray some more and life still doesn't turn out the way you wanted. And sometimes it does. There's a time for everything.

It's what you do with your circumstances that matters. God never causes suffering, but He can sure turn it into something good. Someone said, "God never wastes a trial," and I think that's true.

In the Bible, there's a verse that says God is in the dark clouds. It's easy to think of God as the silver lining, but He is also in the dark clouds. He shines from out of the darkness, which means He takes it over. He works all things together for His good purpose, and His good purpose is always what's best for us. There are a lot of things in my life I might've done different, but if I'd done 'em different, I wouldn't have had the life I've had with my family, music, and friends.

When you surrender your sorrows and struggles to God, you allow the Holy Spirit to teach you through what you suffer. This makes you stronger so you can get through the next hard time and so you can help others along the way. Trials build your character, but only if you want your character built. You can decide to be bitter, but you'll be missing out on so much good. God can send you an idea or change your perspective to turn things around. He can protect you through the storms. Whatever you may be suffering, big or small, I hope that it turns into an opportunity for a miracle today.

## PRAYER FOR TODAY

Lord, I pray that every challenge I face
today will only help me have more of
Your character in me. Amen.

# LYRICS
## "BEST THING THAT EVER HAPPENED"

We talked about all the things we'd do together
How we could buy some land and build a happy home
There was nothing in this world that we loved better
Than makin' plans that never could go wrong

[Chorus]
*As the mem'ries fade away*
*I hardly ever think about you*
*My heart is getting stronger every day and every night*
*When I finally get over you*
*I'll stop cryin' and I'll start laughin'*
*The best thing that ever happened was goodbye*

At first I thought my dreams had all been shattered
But lookin' back I see the truth about your lies
And the sun just keeps on shinin' here without you
I guess broken hearts don't stand the test of time

[Chorus]
*As the mem'ries fade away*
*I hardly ever think about you*
*My heart is getting stronger every day and every night*
*When I finally get over you*
*I'll stop cryin' and I'll start laughin'*
*The best thing that ever happened was goodbye*

[Bridge]
Never thought that I'd like wakin' up without
you by my side
It's sad how I don't miss you anymore most of the time

[Chorus]
*My heart is getting stronger every day and every night*
*I'm gettin' over you*
*I've stopped cryin' and started laughin'*
*The best thing that ever happened was goodbye*

Written by Loretta Lynn and Kim McLean
© Coal Miners Music, Inc./Kim McLean Music

# DEAR UNCLE SAM

You will not fear the terror of the night,
or the arrow that flies by day.

Psalm 91:5

This might be the saddest song I ever wrote. I think music is God's gift to us to help us get through things. Somehow a melody can cry for you. A song can carry away tears that you just can't bear. That's why I wrote this song. I wanted it to cry for all the women who had lost their loved ones to war.

Soldiers defending freedom and the safety of a country's people are the greatest heroes of all, and so are their families who wait back home praying for them every day. We need to keep on prayin' for our soldiers and those who serve this great country. The medical warriors on the front lines helping to save lives need our prayers, too. I know God hates war, but He hates it even worse when innocent people suffer needlessly. We need to help everybody we can when it's in our power to do it.

I think of Jesus as a kind of soldier. He was a soldier of the heart. He took the bullet the devil aimed at me through sin and He died in my place. I will love Him forever for saving me that way.

The Bible tells us to pray for our leaders, and I take

that to mean we should pray for our whole country and those protecting and serving it. We can serve our country through prayer. You can open your Bible right now to Psalm 91 and say a prayer for our soldiers. Psalm 91 is often called "The Soldier's Prayer." I hope it gives you courage for your own life challenges. I especially love the first few verses that say, "You who live in the shelter of the Most High, who abide in the shadow of the Almighty, will say to the Lord, 'My refuge and my fortress: my God, in whom I trust.' For He will deliver you…"

God protects us like a mama bird hiding her chicks under her safe, warm feathers. The children of Israel went through a lot of trials out there in the desert. They faced many battles and fought many wars. A lot of mamas must've lost their husbands and sons. These kinds of things are hard to understand, but there will come a day when wars cease and God's love reigns. We must keep believing and always stand up for what's right.

I pray the Lord bless and keep you and your loved ones today.

## PRAYER FOR TODAY

Lord, I pray for the day when there are no longer any wars in this world. I hold that dream in my heart with You, and I pray that I may be an instrument of Your peace today and every day until our dream comes true. Amen.

# LYRICS
## "DEAR UNCLE SAM"

Dear Uncle Sam I know you're a busy man
And tonight I write to you through tears
with a trembling hand

My darling answered when he got that call from you
You said you really need him but you don't
need him like I do

Don't misunderstand I know he's fighting for our land
I really love my country but I also love my man

He proudly wears the colors of the old
red white and blue
While I wear a heartache since he left me for you
[trumpet]
Dear Uncle Sam I just got your telegram
And I can't believe that this is me shaking like I am
For it said I'm sorry to inform you...

Written by Loretta Lynn
© Sure Fire Music Company, Inc.

# YOU'RE LOOKIN' AT COUNTRY

David danced before the Lord
with all his might.

2 Samuel 6:14

I love how King David was wholeheartedly 100 percent real. He was never a fake and he never apologized for who he was. He was a country boy. He tended sheep in the countryside of Israel and learned all kinds of things out there in the wilderness. He must've fought off bears and wild cats, chiggers and yellow jackets, or ancient Israel's version of them anyway. You learn a lot about life when you grow up in the country, and you don't ever forget those lessons.

Country people have country smarts, and they also have country freedom. We love our makeup and rhinestones, and our Carhartts and fried green tomatoes, and what other people think about that is their business. It's important to love who you are and know what you love. Every one of us is one of a kind.

David was one of a kind. He didn't let anybody persuade him away from loving the Lord with all his might. I wonder if people thought he was crazy dancing so freely in the temple. That was probably against the religious rules, but his heart was so overcome with joy he couldn't help it. It's great to love God so much that you don't care what other people think about it. It's an honest heart that will eventually draw respect from the same people who once criticized you.

I'm proud to be a country girl because I'm God's country girl. If Jesus was on this earth now, I think He might like to come to Nashville and walk a mile or two in my boots. I think He might be proud of me, and I know that if you're doing your best to live for Him, then He's proud of you, too. You don't need to spend too much time worrying about what people think of you. Just celebrate who you are. I know God does!

If you're lookin' at me, you really are lookin' at country, but you're also lookin' at a child of God who loves Him more than anything. I'm proud to be God's country girl!

# PRAYER FOR TODAY

Lord, I know I don't always fit everybody's
mold, but I fit who You created me
to be. Thank You for the gifts You've
given me. Thank You that my greatest joy
is also what brings the greatest
blessings to others. Amen.

# LYRICS
## "YOU'RE LOOKIN' AT COUNTRY"

Well I like my lovin' done country style and this
little girl would walk a country mile
To find her a good ole slow talkin' country boy
I said a country boy
I'm about as old fashioned as I can be and I hope
you're likin' what you see

[Chorus]
*Cause if you're lookin' at me you're lookin' at country*

You don't see no city when you look at me cause
country's all I am
I love runnin' barefoot through the old cornfields
and I love that country ham
Well you say I'm made just to fit your plans
But there's a barnyard shovel fit your hands

[Chorus]
*If your eyes are on me you're lookin' at country*

This here country is a little green and there's a lotta
country that you ain't seen
I'll show you around if you'll show me a weddin' band
I said a weddin' band
When it comes to love well I know about that country
folks all know where it's at

[Chorus]
*If you're lookin' at me you're lookin' at country*
*You don't see no city*
*If your eyes are on me you're lookin' at country*

Written by Loretta Lynn
© Sure Fire Music Company, Inc.

# THE LORD'S PRAYER

Your Kingdom come. Your will be done,
on earth as it is in heaven.
Matthew 6:10

I love "The Lord's Prayer." I love the way so many people have prayed those same words throughout history, starting with Jesus. I hope we never stop praying the words of Christ. We have so much to learn from such a short prayer. All those well-meaning saints who pray long prayers before supper while your food's gettin' cold could learn a thing or two from our Savior!

He starts with "Our Father who art in Heaven," and in two little words—"Our Father"—we are reminded that we all have the same Father. We're all connected to the heart of God. He is sovereign and He should be respected. In this prayer, there is trust that God will provide our basic needs. There is forgiveness and the reminder to forgive the people who have hurt us. There is hope for overcoming our temptations. But my favorite part is when we pray for God's will to be done on earth as it is in Heaven. Have you ever thought about that? If God is answering that prayer, then His will must be gettin' done on earth just like it is in Heaven. Earth echoes Heaven. Right here, right now.

Sometimes we focus more on what's wrong in the world than what's right. It's understandable. But what if you look for love everywhere? What if you start noticing all the ways Jesus's prayer is getting answered every day in your life and in the world around you? It must be true because God answers every prayer. Jesus said that if we ask God for bread, He will not give us a stone. God doesn't tease us with empty promises.

The kingdom of God is a metaphor for a way of the heart, an attitude, a perspective, and it comes every day in our hearts and our individual lives, if we want it. If we each pray for God's will to be done in our lives, all our lives will add up. Jesus is the King of my heart. Maybe everyone doesn't see it yet, but He is also the King of the world.

Did you know that there are two "Lord's Prayers" in the Bible? John 17 is the other Lord's prayer. The whole chapter is in red letters—if you have a red-letter Bible. That just means they printed all of the words Jesus said in red. In John 17, Jesus prayed for us. He asked God to bless His disciples and friends and prayed for everyone who would come to know Him through their testimony. So that includes us. From generation to generation, the story goes on. Jesus prayed that God would protect us and give us complete joy. He asked His Father to make us one with God as He was one with God, which is where the complete joy begins and ends. Isn't that amazing to know that Jesus prayed for you?

## PRAYER FOR TODAY

Father, let Your kingdom come through
me today, and let Your will be done on
earth as it is in Heaven. Amen.

# LYRICS
## "THE LORD'S PRAYER"

Our Father Who art in Heaven
Hallowed be Thy name

Thy kingdom come Thy will be done
On earth as it is in Heaven

Give us this day our daily bread
And forgive us our trespasses as we forgive those
who trespass against us

Lead us not into temptation
But deliver us from evil

For Thine is the kingdom and the power
and the glory forever
Amen.

# DAY 21

# BARGAIN BASEMENT DRESS

Religion that is pure and undefiled
before God, the Father, is this: to care for
orphans and widows in their distress.

James 1:27

Have you ever had anybody buy you a cheap dress? Or a cheap anything? It feels worse than if they'd bought you nothing at all. You can tell when a gift is given from the heart, or when it is given out of guilt or obligation or manipulation. I wrote this song, "Bargain Basement Dress," about that, because I don't like it when women are treated second class. I don't like it when anybody is treated like they don't matter. I believe we all ought to treat each other with dignity, and if somebody is down and out, we ought to love them all the more. James says *that's* true religion.

My favorite book of the Bible is the book of James. He doesn't cut any corners with his faith. If you love God, then you love people, and if you love God and people, it shows by your actions. They say actions speak louder than words, but I want my actions *and* my words to speak love. Words are powerful, and what you go around saying about people exposes your own heart. James talks about that, too. He says you ought to control your tongue because it's like the rudder of a big ship and can steer everything the wrong way.

True religion is wholehearted, whole-life religion. It's not about getting the rules right; it's about loving with the heart of God. It starts with knowing how special you are to God, because *you can't give something you ain't got.* If you want to love people, you have to love yourself. Otherwise, you'll be fakin' it, and that's no good.

The prophet Isaiah wrote that we are a crown of beauty to the Lord, and it's no bargain basement crown, either! God wants to give you His very best every day. That way you can give your very best, too.

## PRAYER FOR TODAY

Lord, open my eyes to see myself the way
You see me so that I can love others the
way You love them. Amen.

# LYRICS
## "BARGAIN BASEMENT DRESS"

Well on a Friday night you draw your pay
and you take in the town
You leave me at home just to lose my mind
while you're out messin' around
But it's four in the morning and you stagger in
and you sure look a mess
With a smile on your face and outstretched arms
and a bargain basement dress

[Chorus]
*I wouldn't wear that dress to a dogfight if that fight was free*
*And the bargain basement dress ain't enough*
*To get your arms around me*
*Well you say when a man works hard all week*
*He deserves to play or rest*
*But honey that ain't right so get out of my sight*
*With that bargain basement dress*

[Chorus]

*I wouldn't wear that dress to a dogfight if that fight was free*
*And the bargain basement dress ain't enough*
*To get your arms around me*
*Well I took all I'm a gonna take and I'm a leavin'*
*you the rest*
*Tell you what I'll do I'll just give you that bargain*
*basement dress*

[TAG]

*Tell you what I'll do I'll just give you that old*
*Bargain basement dress*

Written by Loretta Lynn
© Sure Fire Music Company, Inc.

# DAY 22

# STILL WOMAN ENOUGH

⚮

Esther put on her royal robes and stood
in the inner court of the king's palace.
Esther 5:1

Only two books of the Bible are named for women, Ruth and Esther. Maybe that's because the Lord knew that two women can stir things up more than a hundred men!

Esther was a young Hebrew woman who lived during a time when the Jews were being persecuted by a Persian emperor. She was an orphan who became a queen. It's easy to only see the happy ending when you look at a woman like Esther and assume that everything went her way. But Esther had every excuse in the world to give up on big dreams. Her parents died when she was little, so her cousin Mordecai took her in and raised her as a daughter.

One day, the king threw a seven-day banquet. There were white cotton curtains and blue hangings tied with cords, purple rings and marble pillars, and wine flowing like a river from golden goblets. The king was showing off his wealth and power, and he called for his wife, Vashti, to show her off. She was his trophy, but I guess she didn't like being bossed around, so she refused to go to the party. The king was furious. His officials told him he should get rid of such a disobedient wife. It's hard to blame Vashti for having a mind of her own. Instead, the king banished Vashti, and they had a cattle call of all the young available women in the kingdom. Mordecai sent Esther to be in the running. She had to hide her Jewish identity, but she couldn't hide her beauty. They took her to the makeup artists and stylists of the day to accentuate the positives, and when she was presented to the king, he preferred her out of all those pretty girls. Esther became the queen.

Esther was every bit as stubborn as Vashti, but she was smarter about things. She was grateful for the good life she'd come into, but she didn't forget about her people. The day came when another evil man who worked for the king, Haman, came up with a plan to kill all the Jewish people once and for all, but the Bible says Mordecai knew Esther had been made queen *for such a time as this.* He got word to her about what was happening to her people outside the palace walls. Esther knew what she had to do. She would go to the king on their behalf, knowing that this was against the law with a penalty of death. "If I perish, I perish," she said.

The first thing she did was to pray in the form of fasting. Then she threw a party of her own and showed up with a radiant smile that the king couldn't resist. He offered her half his kingdom, but instead she asked for her people to be set free. The king had that ole Haman put to death on the same gallows Haman had built to hang Mordecai.

Queen Esther is still a revered character today because she stood up for herself and her people with wisdom and grace. We learn a lot from this story. Men, stand up for your women and listen to them. Women, don't try to fight like a man. Your strength is in the beauty God put within you.

## PRAYER FOR TODAY

Lord, please help me to know my true
worth, and help me to use the gifts You
have given me to be a blessing
to others. Amen.

# LYRICS
## "STILL WOMAN ENOUGH"

Well, I've been through some bad times
Been on the bottom, been at the top
And I've seen life from both sides
It's what you make with what you've got
There's been times life's got me down
Picked myself up and bounced right
back around
I wasn't raised to give up
And to this day, you know what?

[Chorus]
*I'm still woman enough*
*Still got what it takes inside*
*I know how to love, lose and survive*
*Ain't much I ain't seen and I ain't tried*
*Been knocked down but never out of the fight*
*I'm strong but I'm tender*
*Wise but I'm tough*

*And let me tell you when it comes to love*
*I'm still woman enough*

I was raised in Oklahoma
Hey, I'm country proud to say
I've seen a lot of changes
Oh, but I ain't never changed
Well, this here girl's been there and done that
They call me hillbilly but I got the last laugh
Standing here today proving in every way

[Chorus]
*I'm still woman enough*
*Still got what it takes inside*
*I know how to love, lose and survive*
*Ain't much I ain't seen and I ain't tried*
*Been knocked down but never out of the fight*
*I'm strong but I'm tender*
*Wise but I'm tough*
*And let me tell you when it comes to love*
*I'm still woman enough*

The years may come and go but for me it's just time
'Cause without a doubt I know it ain't your age
It's a state of mind

[Chorus]
*I'm still woman enough*
*Still got what it takes inside*
*I know how to love, lose and survive*
*Ain't much I ain't seen and I ain't tried*
*Been knocked down but never out of the fight*
*I'm strong but I'm tender*
*Wise but I'm tough*
*And let me tell you when it comes to love*
*I'm still woman enough*

[TAG]
And let me tell you when it comes to love
I'm still woman enough
Still woman enough

Written by Loretta Lynn and Patsy Lynn Russell
© Coal Miners Music, Inc./PatsyLRussell Music

# IF I COULD HEAR MY MOTHER PRAY

Mary treasured all these words
and pondered them in her heart.

Luke 2:19

I wonder what it was like to be Jesus's mother? There must have been quite a few ordinary days like other mothers have, like teaching Him to walk or watching Him play with His friends. It was Mary who let the cat out of the bag about her Son when she had Him turn the water to wine at the wedding in Cana, according to the Gospel of John. She'd been pondering a lot of things in her heart, like that vision of Gabriel when she first learned she was to conceive the Son of God; or the way her twelve-year-old son was teaching the scholars in the square one day; or the way those scholars actually listened to what He had to say! Mary had seen how incredible her Son was long before the rest of Jerusalem knew. Mamas know.

I can just imagine Mary prayin' for Jesus. In those quiet moments on her knees, not yet knowing what He would go through later, she probably didn't think about the fact that He was God. She and Joseph were His earthly parents, entrusted by the Lord to take care of Jesus. When He climbed trees, or worked with tools in the woodshop, or had His first crush, she must have prayed. *Lord, keep Him safe. Lord, keep Him in line with Your plans for His life.* Maybe Mary knew the story in the book of Job from her Hebrew Bible, and how Job prayed that his children would be sanctified. Maybe she whispered the priestly prayer to Him, since as a woman in those times and in that place, she would not have been allowed to pray in public. "Lord, bless Him and keep Him. Lift Your countenance upon Him and be gracious to Him. Make Your face shine upon Him and give Him peace." Maybe the Good Lord chose Mary to be His mother because He knew she would pray faithfully for His son.

My mother prayed like she expected all of Heaven was listening, especially God. And He did. He showed her things in the Spirit. But most importantly, her prayin' taught me how to pray. She didn't just tell me how to pray: she *showed* me. I hope I've shown my kids how to have a heart for God that way. It doesn't stop just because they grow up. A mama can pray and bless her children her whole life long, and I plan to be loving mine all the way from Heaven someday. Two of my kids are already up there waiting for me, and I can't wait to see 'em.

If you're missing your mother today because she's in Heaven, or if you're a mama or a daddy missing your child, my heart goes out to you. I've been through it, too.

When you love somebody, you want to talk to them, and that's all prayin' is—talking to God. Tell Him what's on your mind today.

## PRAYER FOR TODAY

Lord, You told us to honor our father and
our mother. In this world, people don't
always know how special their parents are.
Heal our world and our families. Restore
respect. Give mothers and fathers the
courage to live out their faith so it blesses
the generations to come. Amen.

# LYRICS
## "IF I COULD HEAR MY MOTHER PRAY"

How sweet and happy seem those days of
which I dream
When memory recalls them now and then
And with what rapture sweet my weary
heart would beat
If I could hear my mother pray again

[Chorus]
*If I could hear my mother pray again*
*If I could only hear her tender voice as then*
*How happy I would be*
*Would mean so much to me*
*If I could hear my mother pray again*

She used to pray that I on Jesus would rely
And always walk the shining gospel way
So trusting still His love I'll seek that home above
Where I shall meet my mother some sweet day

[Chorus]

*If I could hear my mother pray again*
*If I could only hear her tender voice as then*
*How happy I would be*
*Would mean so much to me*
*If I could hear my mother pray again*

Written by John Whitfield Vaughan (public domain)

# DAY 24

# ADAM'S RIB

◦◦◦

He who loves his wife loves himself.

Ephesians 5:28

Me and Doo got married young and we both had so much to learn about life, ourselves, and each other. A lot of people misunderstand the Bible when it says, "Wives, obey your husbands." It doesn't leave it there. It says a husband ought to love his wife the way Christ loves the Church. That's BIG love. God never wanted a woman to be a slave to a man; he wanted the man and the woman to be partners in life. Marriage is about serving one another. It's about love and respect for each other. All couples ought to live that way.

When you read a verse in the Bible, it is important to read what came before and after that verse. If you just pick out one verse like "wives, obey your husbands," it's like walking up on a conversation. If you don't know the whole story, you draw the wrong conclusion. Jesus always respected women. He talked to them and took time to listen. He lived in a culture that did not respect women, but Jesus came to teach us how to do things differently, with kindness.

In Ephesians 5, the apostle Paul is clear about how

husbands should honor their wives just like wives honor their husbands. But the picture is bigger than that. Families represent humanity, and all humans should serve one another with dignity and grace.

We all know the story about how woman was created from Adam's rib, but we were all created from God's love. That's the most important thing to know and live by.

## PRAYER FOR TODAY

Lord, help me to know my value and the value of every person as Your precious child. Bring people into my life who will treat me with love and respect, the kind I give back to them. Amen.

# LYRICS
## "ADAM'S RIB"

They say woman was made to please a man
Hey, forget that line, Leroy
If Adam was meant to play around
Then he'd have made Eve a toy
A little wind-up doll that don't run down
And never gets a headache like we do
The reason Adam didn't have a little madam
on the side
The Good Lord didn't make him two

[Chorus]
*Adam's rib to woman's lib*
*We've come a long way*
*From a cookin' and a rockin' the crib*
*This is my night out*
*Don't know what I'll do*
*The Good Lord only knows what I'll get into*

*Well, I won't go as far as some of 'em do*
*But hang in there, girls*
*Cause we ain't through*
*The Lord made man, and man made his woman*
*To do what he wanted her to*

Hey, hey girls, we're catchin' up with him
Lord, it's good for us and it's good for them
It's from workin' hard and workin' late
If there's lovin' on his mind
He'll just have to wait

[Chorus]
*Adam's rib to woman's lib*
*We've come a long way*
*From a cookin' and a rockin' the crib*
*This is my night out*
*Don't know what I'll do*
*The Good Lord only knows what I'll get into*
*Well, I won't go as far as some of 'em do*

*But hang in there, girls*
*Cause we ain't through*
*The Lord made man, and man made his woman*
*To do what he wanted her to*

Written by Loretta Lynn
© Coal Miners Music, Inc./Sure Fire Music Company, Inc.

# DAY 25

# MY LOVE

Many waters cannot quench love,
neither can floods drown it.

Song of Solomon 8:7

The most romantic book in the Bible is the Song of Solomon. It is a beautiful love song. I think God loves it when people fall in love. He made true love so that we could be happy on this earth. You can't always help who you fall in love with. It has to happen naturally. You should never try to talk yourself into being in love with someone, because if it isn't real, it won't last.

God loves us with the "I can't help it" kind of love. That's because He *is* love and He made us. His love is unconditional. Nothing can change it or shake it or make it go away. You can disappoint God, and you don't have to love Him back, but you can't stop Him from loving you.

Songwriters love to use nature imagery to describe love. Maybe Solomon had that idea first when he said, "Many waters cannot quench love." It's natural to describe love with rivers, and stars, and the moon, and the ocean—things only God can make.

Love songs make me think of God, just like the Song of Solomon does. God is my Love. My First Love. My

True Love. It's a love that goes deeper than romance. It's deeper than anything. The miracle of it all is that the love that holds the whole world together comes from the same source as the simplest, most perfect feeling in my heart.

God wants to be your True Love, too. He wants you to know that you matter, that you are worthy of His love, and as important to Him as the moon and all the stars.

# PRAYER FOR TODAY

Lord, thank You that even though You love
everybody in the world the same, You make
me feel like You love me the most. Lord,
I want everybody to know this kind of love.
Help me to show Your love so much that
everybody I meet today wants to
know You, too. Amen.

# LYRICS
## "MY LOVE"

His sweet caress
His tenderness
His warm embrace
His gentle face
I love him so
I'll let him know
That he's my love

Oh moon up there
Show him I care
Give him my love
Oh moon above
He'll always be
The one for me
'Cause he's my love

Oh moon up there

Show him I care

Give him my love

Oh moon above

He'll always be

The one for me

'Cause he's my love, love, love, love

Written by Loretta Lynn

© Sure Fire Music Company, Inc.

# NEW RAINBOW

And the one seated there looks like jasper
and carnelian, and around the throne is
a rainbow that looks like an emerald.

Revelation 4:3

If John were alive today, I think he might be a song-writer. He's so creative and he sees in pictures. He sees Christ with a rainbow around His throne. It's such a beautiful image. Rainbows stand for promises, and if ever the Good Lord made a promise and kept it, it was through Jesus.

According to the Bible, John, who wrote the Gospel of John, also wrote Revelation. A lot of people don't like to read the book of Revelation. They think it is scary, but why would anything in the Bible be scary? God's Word was sent to us as encouragement, so if we find it scary, it's probably because we don't quite understand what we're reading. Revelation is a certain genre of writing called "apocalyptic" writing, intended to be allegory. It helps us through hard times when we can tell the story in a creative and symbolic way. I understand it because I'm a songwriter, and we work through hard times the same way.

Revelation is so colorful and interesting, full of creatures and dragons and crystal seas—and rainbows!

Everything comes full circle in Jesus, even Noah's rainbow. The end of Revelation gives a beautiful description of Heaven, and I think that if God gave John a glimpse of glory, He must do the same for anyone else who might like to "see." I like to say I want people to bring me my flowers before I die. I'd also like to catch a few glimpses of Heaven before I get there. I'm pretty sure I already have. When I sing, when I pray, when I'm taking in the sunshine or talking to my kids and grandkids and the people I love, I see a little bit of Heaven.

Now and then I see a rainbow come over my ranch in Hurricane Mills and I know God is reminding me that there is always hope. The dark clouds and storms of life can hide the rainbows for a while, but we have to remember that the sunlight is always behind those clouds waiting to surprise us with joy again. God doesn't always take away the storms, but He always helps us through them. You can focus on the hardship, or you can focus on the promise of a better day. I've learned this over and over again. You have to keep on the sunny side in your heart and mind. Then you can get through anything. Not long ago, we had a terrible flood on my ranch and in the towns around my Tennessee home. I lost a dear friend in that flood. He was trying to save our animals from gettin' trapped in the raging waters. It broke my heart, and everybody else's heart around here, too. That flood brought devastation to a lot of folks. Then everybody started helpin' everybody. When these things happen, people cry together, work together, and more people pray. I miss my friend who drowned, and I want to honor his memory by appreciating the time I have left on this earth and appreciating the people around me.

A rainbow only happens when there's been rain. You can't have one without the other, and you can't have life without death. Or maybe you can in a way. What we think of as death is just crossing over to eternal life with God. The Bible says there will be no more tears in Heaven, no darkness, and no need for the sun. Heaven must be full of rainbows that never fade.

## PRAYER FOR TODAY

Lord, open my eyes today to see You
everywhere, and help me realize that You
want to grant us reasonable happiness in
this life, and supreme happiness in the next.
Thank You that You are with us now just
like You will be forever. Amen.

# LYRICS
## "NEW RAINBOW"

There's a new rainbow in the sky
I can see the starlight in your eyes
Those love beams shine from cupid's bow
I'm in love with you I know


[Chorus]
I've been searchin' all around to find
someone like you
And now I'm gonna settle down, I've found
someone that's true
That rainbow will never fade away
For I know our love is here to stay


You put a rainbow in my heart
I know you won't tear it apart
And if you say you love me too
Then our dreams will all come true

[Chorus]
I've been searchin' all around to find
someone like you
And now I'm gonna settle down I've found
someone that's true
That rainbow will never fade away
For I know our love is here to stay

Written by Loretta Lynn
© Sure Fire Music Company, Inc.

DAY 27

# WOULDN'T IT BE GREAT

The wolf shall live with the lamb,
the leopard shall lie down with the kid,
the calf and the lion and the fatling
together, and a little child shall lead them.

Isaiah 11:6

We always hope for the best. I think that's a good thing. Never give up hope, and sometimes, hoping for the best seems impossible. The Bible says that with God, all things are possible. That's a nice thought when you think something probably won't happen, but it *could* or *it might*. But what about when something really is *impossible*? Isaiah dreams of a day when a lamb and a leopard will rest together and the lamb won't become the leopard's supper. Are *all* things *really* possible with God?

The most impossible things seem to happen in relationships. You can't make somebody change their ways if they don't want to, and you can't make them love you. Even God can't do that. A lot of people don't love Him, but the important thing is that God loves them anyway, all the time, no matter what. But He also wants people to be decent to one another, and I think it breaks His heart when we're not.

Wouldn't it be great if there were no more addictions and habits that destroy lives and families? Wouldn't it be nice if everybody could love the way God does, with unconditional love? And what if there were no diseases and no wars? We all daydream about these things from time to time. Do you think life would be boring without the challenges? I guess I don't mind an occasional traffic jam, but I'm holding out hope for a healed and happy soul for the whole world.

## PRAYER FOR TODAY

Lord, I'm not giving up on people or on the hope for a better world. Help me to do my part today with You, with prayer and music and kindness. Thank You that You have never given up on me. Amen.

# LYRICS
## "WOULDN'T IT BE GREAT"

Wouldn't it be fine if you could say you love me
just one time with a sober mind?
Wouldn't that be fine, now wouldn't that be fine?

Wouldn't it be great if you could love me first
and let the bottle wait?
Now wouldn't that be great, now wouldn't
that be great?

[Chorus]
*Wouldn't it be great, hey, hey, wouldn't that be great?*
*Throw the old glass crutch away and watch it break*
*Wouldn't it be great, hey, hey, wouldn't that be great?*
*Lord, it's for our sake, now wouldn't that be great?*

In the name of love, what's the man so great
Keep thinking of, in the name of love,
what a man he was

Love went to waste when the sexy lace
couldn't turn his face
The bottle took my place, love went to waste

[Chorus]
*Wouldn't it be great, hey, hey, wouldn't that be great?*
*Throw the old glass crutch away and watch it break*
*Wouldn't it be great, hey, hey, wouldn't that be great?*
*Lord, it's for our sake, now wouldn't that be great?*

*Wouldn't it be good? And I know you could if you just would*
*Wouldn't that be good? Lord, I know you could*

*Wouldn't it be great, hey, hey, wouldn't that be great?*
*Throw the old glass crutch away and watch it break*
*Wouldn't it be great, hey, hey, wouldn't that be great?*
*Lord, it's for our sake, now wouldn't that be great?*

[TAG]
*Now wouldn't that be great?*

Written by Loretta Lynn
© Coal Miners Music, Inc./Sure Fire Music Company, Inc.

167

DAY 28

# WORLD OF FORGOTTEN PEOPLE

God heard their groaning, and God
remembered his covenant with Abraham,
Isaac, and Jacob. God looked upon the
Israelites, and God took notice of them.

Exodus 2:24–25

Nobody hurts alone, but everybody feels alone when they hurt. That's just the way it goes. The truth is, we live in a world of forgotten people. It's important to remember how much we need each other. When you hurt bad enough, you reach out for help, and when you reach out for help, you give another person the chance to love you. More importantly, you find out how loved you are. And there's a kind of hurt that's so hard you can't breathe. It cuts to the depths of your soul. I wish nobody had to go through that kind of hurt, but some of us do. It doesn't matter whether you're rich or poor, famous or quietly known, or what country you're from—too many broken hearts change a person.

Jesus felt forgotten when He died on the cross. He said so. "My God, my God, why have You forsaken me?" And it looked like He'd been forsaken—then He rose from the grave with a resurrection that brought hope to the world of forgotten people. Jesus was God's way of saying, "I've never forgotten you."

We all have days when we think nobody remembers

us or what we've been through. Life goes on past the pain. You cry, you talk it through, and then you move on. You hold a place in your heart for the part of your life or yourself that you had to leave behind, but you have to go on with life. You owe it to yourself and to the people who are still here to love you and be loved by you. Hold on to what you know in your heart. Hold on to the beautiful soul you are. And when that feels impossible, hold on to God.

God cannot forget you. Ever. You are the apple of His eye and that's a promise. He's seen every tear and cried every one of them with you. The Bible says God keeps our tears in His bottle. Maybe He uses those salty tears to keep the oceans full and bring new beauty and life to the world. Just remember over and over that He will make you strong again. The Bible promises that when we are the weakest, God is our strength. Let Him comfort you. Let Him heal you. Let Him remember what you went through and let Him lead you on with new joy.

Your joy will heal others who are still hurting. Your story will help others know that they are not forgotten.

## PRAYER FOR TODAY

Lord, I don't want to be a forgotten person.
Please remember me today with grace,
with compassion, with kindness, and with
love. Please surprise me with joy. Amen.

# LYRICS
# "WORLD OF FORGOTTEN PEOPLE"

[Chorus]
*I live in a world, world of forgotten people*
*Who loved and lost their hearts so many times*
*I'm here in a world, world of forgotten people*
*Where every heart is achin' just like mine*

Well I've loved and I've been loved but I had
a reckless heart
And the many dreams I had torn apart
Now I find that I was wrong too late I'm all alone
Alone in a world of broken hearts

[Chorus]
*I live in a world, world of forgotten people*
*Who loved and lost their hearts so many times*
*I'm here in a world, world of forgotten people*
*Where every heart is achin' just like mine*

Written by Loretta Lynn
© Sure Fire Music Company, Inc.

## DAY 29

# WHO SAYS GOD IS DEAD?

Jesus said to him, "I am the way and the truth and the life. No one comes to the Father except through me."

John 14:6

You can't believe everything you hear, and I heard a doozy one time. Word was spread around that God was dead. At first it sounded ridiculous, like a sad joke. Who would say God is dead? It's like saying fire isn't warm and the sun isn't hot, only worse and even more absurd. It's sad to think that some people get swayed by headlines like that.

I can see it now…I'm sitting at the kitchen table talking to Jesus when somebody walks in and says God is dead…and me and Jesus look at each other and bust out laughing. That's how I felt in my soul when I heard there was a new kind of movement declaring God dead. An atheist philosopher came up with the idea and spread it around, but I just couldn't keep my mouth shut about it. That's why I wrote this song.

God loves atheists, too, and lucky for them, God can't die. God *is* life. Jesus said, "I am the way and the truth and the life." My believing that doesn't make it so. It just *is*. But my believing it makes life make sense. It rings true. That's because God created us, and He created us to love us and for us to love Him. Everybody has a God-shaped hole in their heart that only God can fill.

The rumor that God is dead can't hurt God's reputation. People who know Him, know Him. You can tell me water ain't wet, but that won't change what I know to be true. But don't tell me God is dead, because it breaks my heart to think anyone would say that about my best friend. He is always present with me, and He's always present with you.

When the world goes against your faith, stand firm. Let the whole world know that you know who is holding this whole beautiful mess together!

# PRAYER FOR TODAY

Lord, You stick up for me all the time, and I can't help but stick up for You. You are so good, and I want to be an expression of Your love in this world. Help me to love those who don't know You. Help me to love them like You do, so that I might be a testimony. Amen.

# LYRICS
## "WHO SAYS GOD IS DEAD?"

Who says God is dead, I'm talking to Him now
Who says God is dead, He's with us all right now
He knows ever move that you make
He knows ever time you make a mistake
The rumor has been spread
Who says God is dead

Who says God is dead, that's stooping mighty low
I'd like to meet 'em face to face and tell 'em it's not so
I've got my Savior by the hand
He's a leadin' me to the Promised Land
No, I'm not outta my head
Who says God is dead

Who says God is dead, He's a watching you right now
Who says God is dead, He's a reaching for you now

If I were you I'd kneel and pray
'Cause we're not promised one more day
Remember blood was shed, who says God is dead
Who says God is dead
Who says God is dead
Who says God is dead

Written by Loretta Lynn
© Sure Fire Music Company, Inc.

# I'D RATHER HAVE JESUS

Whom have I in heaven but you?
And there is nothing on earth that
I desire other than you.

Psalm 73:25

People want a lot of things. Cars. Homes. Horses. Guitars. Fancy clothes. I have all those things, but if you told me I could have those things or Jesus, I'd keep Jesus. The good news is that we don't have to make that choice, not literally anyway. But you *do* have to make that choice in your heart.

I'm not sure how people get the idea that they have to live an either/or life, when God has always blessed His people with a both/and life. We think, "I can either be a good Christian, *or* have nice things." The truth is you can be a good Christian *and* have nice things. I know how a person can get that backward. Somebody messed up our thinkin' when they said money was the root of all evil and left it at that. It's loving money more than God or using people and steppin' on 'em to get more money that is evil. Greed is the root of evil, not money itself. There wouldn't be so many poor people if there weren't so many people greedy about money and turning it into an idol. Jesus taught again and again that it is the attitude in your heart that makes the difference. Good and evil begin with the intentions of a person's heart. The richest person in the world could be a saint, and the poorest person could be a devil.

The Bible has a lot more to say about the blessings of money than it does the evil of it. He anointed kings and made them wealthy. King Solomon was one of the wealthiest people in all of history. Job was wealthy because of God's blessing, then poor, then rich again. Esther and Ruth both became wealthy because of God's blessing. And the apostle Paul wrote to the Ephesians that God was able to give them abundance beyond what they could even ask or imagine. In Philippians, Paul says that God supplies all our needs according to His riches in glory by Christ Jesus. The Bible says God owns the cattle on a thousand hills.

When you hold Jesus in your heart as the most important thing in your life, your faithfulness to God can line up with God's faithfulness to you. It's like being under the spout where the glory comes out. But you have to attend the feast if you want the fine food. Don't treat

God like a drive-through window. Spend time talking to Him, soaking in His good Word, thinking about Him, and singing to Him. The very first commandment has always been to love the Lord with all your heart. *All* of it. You might think that if your whole heart is full of love for God there won't be any room left, but that's the beauty of our Lord. Loving Him with your whole heart expands your heart to love the way He loves.

I really would rather have Jesus than anything, but I've noticed something so great about that. When you love the Lord more than anything, He gives you everything your heart desires. Your heart gets lined up with His, and you start wanting what God wants. God wants the very best for you. Don't try to figure it all out. Trust Him and focus on the joy of every new day you are given. Love the Lord by doing your best with the work you are given to do. Love the Lord by loving your family and friends. If you stumble, get up and try again. All through the day, when you notice God's presence, tell Him you love Him, heart to heart.

I am prayin' for you, that God will draw you close to Himself, so close that you can hear Him when He guides you in every detail of your life.

## PRAYER FOR TODAY

Lord, I'm not trying to shut out the gifts of this life by loving You the most. You're not an escape hatch; You are a door to all that is good. You put us on this earth to bless us. Please forgive me for the ways I have refused Your blessings without even realizing I was doing it. I open my arms wide to You now because Your arms are open wide for me. Draw me close to Your heart. I love You, Lord. Amen.

# LYRICS
## "I'D RATHER HAVE JESUS"

I'd rather have Jesus than silver or gold
I'd rather be His than have riches untold
I'd rather have Jesus than houses or lands
I'd rather be led by His nail pierced hand

[Chorus]
*Than to be the king of a vast domain*
*Or be held in sin's dread sway*
*I'd rather have Jesus than anything*
*This world affords today*

I'd rather have Jesus than men's applause
I'd rather be faithful to His dear cause
I'd rather have Jesus than worldwide fame
I'd rather be true to His holy name

[Chorus]
*Than to be the king of a vast domain*
*Or be held in sin's dread sway*
*I'd rather have Jesus than anything*
*This world affords today*

He's fairer than lilies of rarest bloom
He's sweeter than honey from out of the comb
He's all that my hungering spirit needs
I'd rather have Jesus and let Him lead

[Chorus]
*Than to be the king of a vast domain*
*Or be held in sin's dread sway*
*I'd rather have Jesus than anything*
*This world affords today*

Written by Rhea F. Miller (public domain)

May the Lord bless you and keep you.
Much love,
Loretta and Kim

# FINAL PRAYER

Lord, I pray for everybody who ever reads
this book. I pray that they would feel a little
closer to You every time they read it, and
that they will always love and follow You.
May the world be kinder, brighter,
and blessed because we wrote these words
and songs, and because somebody read
and listened with their heart.

# A FINAL WORD

It was a joy and a great honor to co-write this book with Loretta. We had just finished our final edits when the Lord took her to her Heavenly home. I know she will be up there smiling with Jesus every time this book blesses someone's soul. Thank you, Loretta. We will miss you.

—*Kimberly*

# ACKNOWLEDGMENTS

We would like to acknowledge the outstanding team of creative professionals who have made this book possible. They caught the vision with us and worked fearlessly to ensure that the heart of this work shines through in every aspect of its process and delivery to the world. Many thanks to:

Jeff Kleinman, Steve Troha, and Sophie Brett-Chin with Folio Literary Management for making this happen. Remarkable. You all are the A-team of book agents, and we are so proud to work with the very best!

Our team at Worthy Publishing:

Gabriella Wikidal, cover designer, for her most excellent cover design. You *can* judge this book by its cover, and we think it's great and will be a beautiful visual on the shelves and digital platforms for many years to come.

Jeana Ledbetter, editor, for her tireless and patient editing and especially her encouragement and appreciation for our writing. She pursued quality in the details, but even more importantly, we knew we were working with a quality person, heart and soul.

Morgan Rickey, editorial assistant, for patiently keeping us on track with deadlines and expectations. We songwriters need people like her to follow us around and remind us that our timeless joy must find a place on the calendar if it's going to do anybody any good in this world.

Stacey Reid, production editor, for keeping the devil out of the details. We had the very best production editor putting the finishing touches on everything and making sure the team efforts came together with perfection.

Cat Hoort, associate marketing director, for making this work set sail. We could write a thousand books, but if nobody knew about them, they'd go nowhere. We have been praying all along that this book will end up in the hands of those who need it. Cat's work will set the stage for years to come.

Laini Brown, publicity, for tooting our horn for us, so to speak. Publicity is such a great tool. It gets people talking, and if you think about it, without that, even Jesus wouldn't be so famous. Our mission is to "Go unto all the world," and we appreciate Laini for helping us spread the *Word*!!!!

Daisy Hutton, publisher, for her incredible insight and foresight as a publisher. The world of books is a lot like the world of music and is competitive and challenging. We are grateful for the opportunity to have a place on the literary landscape.

And finally, Chris Allums, Licensing Director, Kim McLean Music LLC, for his consistent drive for excellence in music publishing. He's a great colleague and a true friend.

Our family, friends, and church community for their unconditional love and support.

We would not be able to get our work done without the support and vision of these great people.

Love to all,

*Loretta and Kim*

# ABOUT THE AUTHORS

**Loretta Lynn** has produced multiple gold albums and boasts an impressive 60-year country music track record, during which she has sold over 45 million albums and produced 16 number-one hit singles and 11 number-one albums. She has received numerous awards for her groundbreaking role in country music, including awards from both the Country Music Association and the Academy of Country Music. She is the most awarded female country recording artist and the only female ACM Artist of the Decade (1970s).

**Kim McLean** is a Grammy-recognized, Dove Award–winning singer-songwriter. Renowned in the industry, she has worked with major labels including Curb and Sony as a music producer and was instrumental in developing a song-writing program at Trevecca University, where she obtained her MA in Religion and Doctorate in Education. In addition to other honors, she has garnered awards from NSAI and ASCAP with TV/film credits on NBC, ABC, and CBS. As an ordained minister, McLean is currently the lead pastor of Music City West Church in Nashville.